Watching Grizzly Bears in North America

Elizabeth Miles

Heinemann Library
Chicago, Illinois

Customer Service 888-454-2279

Visit our website at www.heinemannraintree.com

Designed by Ron Kamen and edesign
Illustrations by Martin Sanders
Printed and bound in China by South China Printing Company

10 09 08 07 06
10 9 8 7 6 5 4 3 2 1

Library of Congress Cataloging-in-Publication Data
Miles, Elizabeth, 1960-
  Watching grizzly bears in North America / Elizabeth Miles.
      p. cm. -- (Wild world)
  Includes bibliographical references and index.
  ISBN 1-4034-7227-0 (lib. bdg. : hardcover : alk. paper) -- ISBN1-4034-7240-8 (pbk. : alk. paper)
  1. Grizzly bear--North America--Juvenile literature. I. Title. II. Wild world (Chicago, Ill.)
  QL737.C27M494 2006
  599.784'097--dc22   2005017346

Acknowledgments
The author and publishers are grateful to the following for permission to reproduce copyright material: Alamy pp. **25** (Curtis Richter), **28** (Franzfoto.com); Ardea pp. **13** (M Watson), **20** (Jean Michel Labat); Corbis pp. **4** (Kennan Ward), **18** (Joe McDonald), **29** (Kennan Ward); Creatas pp. **5** (bottom), **26**, **28**; FLPA pp. **8** (Michio Hoshino), **22** (L Lee Rue), **27** (Michio Hoshino); Getty Images pp. **9**, **14**, **17**; KPT Power Photos p. **7**; NHPA pp. **5** (top T Kitchin & T Hurst),**10** (John Shaw), **12** (Rich Kirchner); PhotoLibrary.com pp. **15** (Konrad Wothe), **23** (Daniel Cox); Science Photo Library p. **11** (William Ervin); Still Pictures p. **19** (Ted Miller); Zefa p. **16** (E & B Bauer); Steve Bloom p. **24**. Cover photograph of grizzly bear with cubs reproduced with permission of Nature Picture Library/Eric Baccega.

The publishers would like to thank Michael Bright for his assistance in the preparation of this book. Every effort has been made to contact copyright holders of any material reproduced in this book. Any omissions will be rectified in subsequent printings if notice is given to the publishers. The paper used to print this book comes from sustainable resources.

Some words are shown in bold, **like this**. You can find out what they mean by looking in the glossary.

Contents

Meet the Grizzlies

This is North America, the home of grizzly bears. Grizzly bears are big brown bears. Bears are strong **mammals** with thick, long fur.

▼ *Some grizzly bears have hairs with white tips that make their fur look grizzled (gray).*

There are nine kinds of bear. They come in different colors and sizes. Grizzly bears, or grizzlies, are the only kind to have a **hump** on their shoulders.

Black bears (above) and polar bears (left) are two other kinds of bear.

5

Where Do Grizzly Bears Live?

North America is a large **continent** with many different types of land. There are deserts, forests, mountains, and valleys. Grizzlies live in mountains and forests.

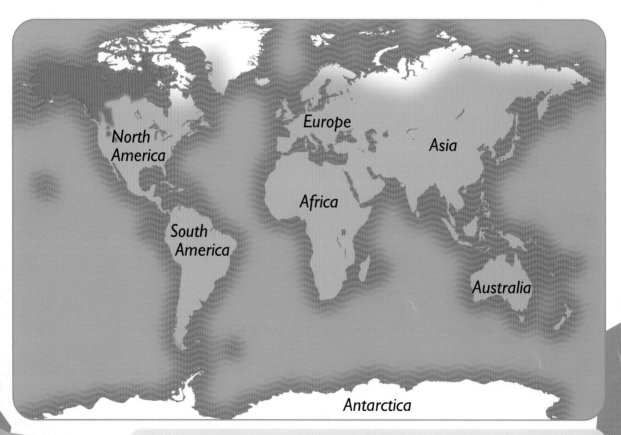

Key ● This color shows where grizzly bears live in North America.

Rivers and streams run down the mountains and hills.

In the mountain areas of North America, there are forests and **meadows**. Lots of trees, bushes, and grasses grow here. Many animals live here, too.

7

There's a Bear!

Grizzlies are not easy to find. Their brown fur makes them hard to see against the land. This grizzly is walking on its four large feet on the grass.

▼ The **hump** on this bear's shoulders tells you it is a grizzly bear.

42 teeth

small round ears

▶▶ *A grizzly bear's claws are twice as long as your finger.*

strong paws

long claws

thick fur

Grizzlies are very large and strong. They must be watched from a safe distance! A large grizzly weighs about the same as six grown-up people.

9

Bear Territory

Most grizzlies like to live alone. They each have a **territory**. It can be as big as a large city. **Male** grizzlies usually stay in the same territory all their life.

⏶ *This grizzly's territory covers **meadows**, woodlands, hills, and streams.*

A male grizzly will fight any other bears that come into its territory. **Female** grizzlies make sure their **cubs** do not wander into male territories.

▲ The grizzly rubs its **scent** on a tree to warn other bears to keep away.

Woodland Food

Grizzlies eat grasses, roots, and animals. In spring, there are many young animals in the woods. The grizzly can kill a young deer with its strong paws.

▶▶ *Instead of killing animals to eat, grizzlies sometimes prefer to find and eat* **carrion**.

In spring and summer, there are lots of **insects** to eat. The grizzly tears the bark off trees with its sharp claws. It can eat the insects hiding underneath.

▶▶ *This grizzly is looking for a meal in this tree.*

Fast or Slow?

Grizzlies may look too big to move fast, but they can run faster than you. A grizzly runs as fast as a car to catch a young deer.

It is hard to escape from a running grizzly.

In spring, fish called salmon **migrate** up the rivers of North America. A grizzly is quick enough to grab a jumping fish with its big front paws.

▲ *This grizzly stands in the river, ready to grab its food.*

Mating

In early summer, the grizzlies get together to **mate**. A **male** grizzly walks up to a **female**. It takes time for the female to accept him.

🔺 *At first, the female grizzly tries to frighten the male away.*

The female bear is much smaller than the male.

The male stays with the female for two weeks. Afterward, the female is **pregnant**. Her **cubs** will not be born until winter comes.

17

In the Heat

In summer, grizzlies shed some of their thick fur, but they still get hot in the sun. On hot days, they will lie in the **shade** to keep cool.

▲ *In mid-summer, the grizzly will go up hills or mountains to find fresh grasses.*

In the summer, grizzlies spend most of their time eating. This grizzly can smell a mouse. It scratches at the ground to get the mouse out of its underground nest.

▼ *The grizzly uses its sharp, curved claws to dig.*

Winter Is Coming

In the fall, the grizzlies get ready for the cold winter ahead. They eat lots of berries to build up their strength. Each bear digs a winter **den**.

⏶ *The grizzly digs its den under a tree because the tree roots make the roof strong.*

When winter comes, there are few berries left. The grasses are covered in snow. It is time for the grizzly to go into its den to sleep.

▲ *The grizzly stays in the den for the winter and is asleep most of the time.*

21

In the Den

After a few months, the **female** grizzly has her **cubs**. The cubs are born in the dark, warm **den**. Outside, it is still snowy and cold.

⬆ ***Newborn*** *cubs have little fur and cannot see or hear.*

The cubs stay in the den and drink their mother's milk. After two months, the cubs have grown bigger. The den gets crowded.

▲ *These cubs are not yet old enough to leave the den.*

Young Cubs

In the spring, the weather is warmer. The young **cubs** leave the **den** for the first time. They are three months old.

▼ To be safe, the young cubs stay close to their mother.

By spring, the cubs are eating the same kind of food as their mother. The cubs play-fight together. This teaches them how to protect themselves.

▽ *Cubs watch their mother. They learn how to find berries and **insects** to eat.*

Grizzlies in Danger

Cubs stay close to their mother for safety. If they wander away, **male** bears or wolves might hunt and kill them.

▶▶ *A wolf can easily catch a bear cub. The cubs cannot run very fast.*

In a few years, the cubs have learned everything they need to know from their mother. They are stronger now. It is time for the cubs to begin life on their own.

*Each young bear sets off to find its own **territory**.*

Tracker's Guide

When you want to watch animals in the wild, you need to find them first. You can look for clues they leave behind.

▲ *A grizzly's paw print shows five toes with long claws.*

◀◀ *Grizzlies leave holes behind where they have been digging for food.*

▶▶ *Sometimes grizzlies leave scratch marks high on a tree.*

29

Glossary

carrion animals that have already died or been killed by another animal

continent the world is split into seven large areas of land called continents. Each continent is divided into different countries.

cub young grizzly bear

den bear's home, often underground or in a cave

female animal that can become a mother when it is grown up. Girls and women are female people.

hump lump on the back

insect small animal with six legs and three main parts to its body. Ants, beetles, and bees are all insects.

male animal that can become a father when it is grown up. Boys and men are male people.

mammal group of animals that feed their babies their own milk and have some hair on their bodies

mate when male and female animals produce young

meadow area where grasses and flowers grow

migrate travel a long distance, following the same journey every year

newborn just been born

pregnant when a female has mated with a male and young are growing inside her

scent smell left by an animal

shade cooler places hidden from the sun by things such as trees or grasses

territory area where an animal lives and feeds

Find Out More

Books

Dineen, Jacqueline. *Grizzly Bears*. Mankato, Minn.: Smart Apple Media, 2003.

Fox, M. *Continents: North America*. Chicago: Heinemann Library, 2002.

Kendell, Patricia. *Grizzly Bears*. Chicago: Raintree, 2003.

Pyers, Greg. *Mountain Explorer*. Chicago: Raintree, 2004.

Pyers, Greg. *Why Am I a Mammal?* Chicago: Raintree, 2005.

Stone, Jason and Jody. *Grizzly Bears*. Woodbridge, Conn.: Blackbirch, 2000.

Swinburne, Stephen R. *Moon in Bear's Eyes*. Honesdale, Pa.: Boyds Mill, 2005.

Index